A Collection of Poems

Martin Turner

Grosvenor House
Publishing Limited

This book is published by
Grosvenor House Publishing Ltd
Link House
140 The Broadway, Tolworth, Surrey, KT6 7HT.
www.grosvenorhousepublishing.co.uk

This book is a work of fiction. Any resemblance to people or events, past or present, is purely coincidental.

A CIP record for this book
is available from the British Library

ISBN 978-1-80381-568-8
eBook ISBN 978-1-80381-627-2

CONTENTS

Introduction

I do not claim to be a poet because
I have never studied or tried to learn
about the different forms poetry can
take. Almost all my work is triggered
by someone or something in my life
and then simply pours from some
deep source in my head. That may be
why I have been accused of never
using one word when nine will do!

It may also explain why this book
is different. I want it to reveal how
even the darkest times that we all
experience can pass and life become
good and fun again. Quite a number
of these poems are about love and were
inspired by love. I have been very
fortunate and I could not be more
grateful to the different muses that
have shared life and love with me
and given me the ability to put down
what I felt. Because of them I have never
had to sit and try to think what to write.
With love you never walk alone.

Martin Turner
May 2023

LOVE CAN TRANSCEND TIME

Love can transcend time.
But when love and life
travel together,
arc across the heavens
and through the years,
a small miracle
has taken place.

Travel with a sure heart
through darkness
and the turbulence
of our time,
and know that
if you think of me
I shall be there,
beside you.

When you think of me,
I shall be there.

In the era of Covid-19, December 2020

FLANDERS' POPPY

Oh Poppy,
you bloodied talisman
of Flanders' Fields
where men did meet
to find their fate.
Your soft, scarlet robes
are a silken shroud
for those who wait
to greet oblivion.

You grow
where men's machines
have torn the tangled earth,
and men themselves
form mud with scornful clay.
You are not blind or deaf
to the anguish of the earth
when scarlet wounds
mock your blooms
as they too
turn to face the sky.
Sun fondles you,
intense with light and warmth,
and, like man's good intentions,
each velvet petal
falls lonely

(Cont.)

to the waiting ground,
full of silent passion.
Your naked head is left,
a tombstone for the world.

Written to accompany my carving, 'Jimmy'
in Sherborne Abbey, 1999

A FALLING LEAF

There is no sound
from a falling leaf
flickering to
the waiting earth.
A falling leaf
cannot sense
its fickle fate,
the earth that waits its kiss
is silent in dark mystery.
Slipping, falling,
how can it know
that, joined at last,
this is how it must be,
and will be,
for ever and ever.

Amen?

LABURNUM COTTAGE

Good morning, Mrs Humby,
how do you do?
I came with Anne to Laburnum Cottage,
your home and sanctuary,
where memories and dreams
have been safely kept.
And where stout stone walls
still breathe peace and constancy.

We worked together, Anne and I,
and in your garden
I looked across the vale
through your eyes
and saw what you have seen,
and tried to hear what you were saying
and what you expected.

It's quite all right,
I know how your garden
was sowed with love and care
and it will be again,
even as those who live there
change like the seasons.
Because what you planted
is still there for those who can see
and understand.

(Cont.)

And you have only moved
from Laburnum Cottage
to rest in the hearts of your children
and those who know you.
Thank you for letting me stay.
I was glad to support your daughter Anne
as she remade your home as you knew it.

Now Laburnum Cottage quietly waits
while, like those seasons,
we shall all come and go.
But you and we have left
part of our spirit in your home
so that it can welcome
the new and give sanctuary
to the dreams of others.
I hope we meet again.

Laburnum Cottage, Kirk Deighton,
Yorkshire, July 2013

DARK CASTLES OF THE MIND

O fatal love,
you bloodied shade of Bluebeard's lair
where lovers meet to cast their bait,
your scarlet gown displays your charms,
reveals your love, and seals your fate.
Red-stained love and lust
reel round these stone-faced walls,
drip mute despair to waiting ground,
full of silent passion.

You willed the light
bleach black ugliness
and melt his mind
to thoughts of grace and love.
But light revealed
a mind impervious to love,
locked in spinning fantasies
of life and death.

Strange, leaning walls, deathly dark,
and shifting doors with rays of light and hope,
both drowned by menace,
black, dank, soaked with fate.
Fear haunts dark doorways of the mind
which taunt with treasures,
but find them and they glitter
with blood and pain.

(Cont.)

The swinging mind cries out
that love can conquer all,
but Nemesis then flirts her fan
And Evil shrieks and tears
his tortured angel - man.

This wheel will turn
until time's circle is closed at eternity.
You, shade of midnight,
shall not rest alone
for you, too, will be haunted
by the shades of other times . . .

March 2002
Written after Duke Bluebeard's Castle
at The Royal Opera House

'TADDIES'

Nibble, nibble,
Wriggle, wriggle,
Under reed and log,
What a lot of growing up
To make a little frog.

Nibble, nibble,
Dibble, dibble,
Big you grow and hale.
Your legs grow strong –
The back ones long,
But look, you have lost your tail!

Nibble, nibble,
Croak, croak,
King of the rushy bog.
Tadpole past
Quite gone, at last,
A happy, hoppy frog.

June 1980

PAINTED UNDER A CLOUD

On this sun-gilt autumn day I ran,
clear across the sweeping down,
past castle, lake and fresh-ploughed land.
Through the stubble,
and the rubble of my values.
You excite and draw my soul,
lift me through the warm, still air
and leave me painted beneath a cloud
to guard you.

October 2000

THE CHERRY TREE

The pale pink petals
of the cherry tree
dance dainty
in the chill east wind.

Time waits
as notes from Schubert's soul
hang sweet, poignant
over the soft-chattering stream.

The daffodils' mute trumpets
mark time,
and heavy bumblebee
moves steadily
from temptation to temptation.

Life's tears
redeem my soul
as petals drift
against the cold, cobalt sky.

A lark climbs
and sings,
the swirl of life
begins again.

Resurrection?

From my studio in Sandford Orcas

WHEN YOU TRAVEL

When you travel over the oceans,
Travel with me.

When you are tired, anxious and fraught,
Travel with me.

When you travel in your thoughts,
Travel with me

In the complex, jewel-inlaid world
that is our life,
Travel with me.

Always,
Travel with me.

A NEW UNIVERSE

My mind swirls,
brewing and bubbling
like a new universe forming,
expanding both good and bad.
Sometimes I wonder if my
feelings and thoughts
will boil over
and, without a place to go,
shatter this thin bone shell.

This morning
the dark ghost of Yetminster
twice paused and slid away,
stirring pain and clouding
a bright Spring day.
And even the daffodils
shook their heads
in the sudden chill.

But I hope with time
my heart can again
be full of happiness,
and trust.
In this new
and real world
my soul will find
its way home.

2010

A SMALL SPIDER FALLS

A small spider falls,
saved by a silken trace.
It is time – in his time,
to set his net
beside dark, unknown waters
and wait his fate.

Summer withdraws
into uncertain autumn.
And fleeting clouds,
outriders of the equinox,
tick the time that leaves,
as we shall leave our time.

Autumn is here,
late with golden glint.
Shadows spread long
as the torch is passed,
and the world
moves on.

The spider climbs
and turns and turns
his artful work.
Priceless, shining jewels
glimpsed by the evening sun
that slips from an immense
and endless sky.

Canal de la Somme, 2006

HEAVENLY BODIES

Your star still sings to me
both night and day
across cold cobalt aeons,
drawn by a power, untouched, unseen,
towards this strange conjunction,
this changing state
of dark and light, of pain and calm,
of love and harm – but never hate.

And I did spy thee
through my 'scope
and thrilled to sense you near.
You spun my world when you did choose
through cloudy mists of hope.
But, if I lost your love in astral time,
my soul would haunt eternity,
seeking still for thine.

THE SONG OF SANDFORD ORCAS

Ye who love a country's legends,
Love the ballads of a people,
That like voices from afar off
Call to us to pause and listen,
Speak in tones so plain and childlike,
Scarcely can the ear distinguish
Whether they are sung or spoken;
Listen to this local legend,
To this song of Sandford Orcas!

Sing O Spirit of the Mitre
Of the happy days that followed
In the land of Sandford Orcas,
In the pleasant land and peaceful!
Sing the mystery of Mervyn,
Sing the blessings of the cornfields!
Buried was the bloody hatchet,
Buried were all warlike weapons.
And the war cry was forgotten –
Tho' the PCC had gathered
And Church changes not forgotten.

There was peace among the neighbours;
Unmolested roved dog-walkers,
Andrea, Alan, Cheryl, Peter,
Down the coombe through stream and river
Chased the deer and killed the pheasants;

(Cont.)

Killed the stupid bloody pheasants.
Unmolested worked the women,
Made their jam like Mary Stewart,
Gathered berries from the hedgerows
Dressed in clothes from Marks and Spencer.

All around the happy village
Stood the maize fields green and shining,
Waved the green plumes of Monsanto,
Waved the soft and sterile tresses
Filling all the air with pollen.

It was the women every Thursday
Led the way to join their neighbours,
Through the tranquil air of evening;
Past the mist among the treetops
From the Vale of Higher Sandford,
From the Ridge of Corton Denham,
From the nearby town of Sherborne,
From the sodden lanes of Trent.

All the folk beheld the signal,
Heard the distant bronze bells ringing,

Pealing from St Nicolas tower.
By this signal from afar off,
Bending like a wand of willow,
Waving like a hand that beckons,
Alan Page the mighty landlord,
Calls the families together,
Calls the village to his council.

(Cont.)

Down the lanes and o'er the meadows
Came the people of the village;
Came the Earls and Mike and Sally,
Came Tom and Mary and the Fareys,
Came the Sherwins; Lorna, Laurie,
Came Liz and Anne; Dave and Andrea.
Came tall McBeath and Rita Virgo,
Came Ian, Steve and Martin Turner
(Steve Rose and Fred were there before them).
Many others drawn together
By the signal of the bronze bells
To the meeting of the like-minds,
To the great white hamstone dwelling.

And they sat there in the bar room
With their torches, men and women,
Painted like the leaves of autumn,
Painted like the sky of morning;
Joy of friends that share together
In that fire that flames the senses.

Alan Page, the mighty landlord,
With his maid, the graceful Cheryl,
Looked upon them with compassion,
With paternal love and pity;
Looked upon their jokes and wrangling
But as quarrels among children,
But as feuds and fights of children!

(Cont.)

Over them he stretched his right hand,
Took their coins and took their orders,
To subdue their stubborn natures,
To allay their thirst and fever,
Till time was called
Or might be, later.

Then the people left quite quietly,
In ones and twos, they took their leave,
Lit a torch as dark descended
That their souls upon their journeys
May not lack the cheerful light,
May not grope in darkness.

'Farewell, noble Alan, Cheryl!
We have put you to the trial,
To the proof have put your patience
By the insult of our presence,
By the outrage of our actions;
We have found you great and noble
Fail not in the greater trial,
Fail not in the harder struggle
For we need you here a while'.

When they ceased, a sudden darkness
Fell and filled the silent inn.
The landlord paused and heard a rustle
As of garments trailed by him;
Heard the curtain of the doorway
Lifted by a hand he saw not,

(Cont.)

Felt the cold breath of the night air,
For a moment saw the starlight;
But he saw the ghosts no longer,
Saw no more the wandering spirits
From the Vale of Sandford Orcas,
From the land of the hereafter.

Written in 1999 at Sandford Orcas.

With apologies to Henry Wadsworth Longfellow – and Hiawatha!

TWO SOULS

Where will it lead
this diamond-crusted way?
We cannot know
but I would travel with you
side by side
until these jewels become the stars
and frosted hedgerows spin themselves
to mists of time,
and fate reveals our destination.

Written following a run on ice-covered roads
near Sandford Orcas in frosty sunshine.

I SIT LIKE A STATUE

I sit like a statue
and contemplate my muse.
But beneath the still, impassive image
I present to the world around me,
my mind and soul spin and whirl,
each struggling for ascendancy.

You, my muse Erato,
are more than the sum
of your qualities.
You inspire dreams
and pass me a lever
to help me move the world.

Convention's chains will shackle love.
Some in our lives
will judge us by what they see,
through a stone veil of unknowing.
But you and I understand how intense
deep feelings and thoughts can be.

Not only my muse
you are a pearl,
warm, lustrous and precious;
studded in the shell of my being.
The world can see my form,
but you have known my soul.

LIFE MAY BUBBLE

Life may bubble
like a summer cloud
drifting with quiet intent
above a dreaming world.
Or it can march
purposefully along determined lines,
baffling the sun's beams,
deceiving with light and dark.

But, as our world
winds its way through time,
I am afraid
of the dark, torn clouds
masking light and warmth
and driven by
senseless squalls of confusion,
that push us towards
an unknown, empty fate.

I wanted to fly
above the clouds
towards the light,
to dance with gods,
but my wings were clipped
by a cold, black blade
that tumbled me
back to earth.

January 2010

ON BEING JETSAM

Here I am,
beached in a dull, scruffy corridor,
cramped in a sticky chair among the
aluminium sticks and frames loosely attached
to the sorry spoils of arthritis
that cannot stand and cannot sit
and cannot walk
to be told decomposition
is inevitable.

Brave bubbles
in the brown wrack
of the here and now
smiling with companions and staff
but living under the torn clouds
that pass across
the sun's light and warmth
driven by the cool indifference
of fate.

Written in the rheumatoid arthritis
waiting room at Yeovil Hospital,
September 2010

ONE

I have not spoken to another
on this empty Sunday.
I work, and play the music
of days when I was young and happy;
when I believed life,
or at least love,
was for ever.

Now those I love,
and those I created,
have their own worlds
to experience and share
with those closest to them.
My soul has lost the path.
And while two men can fight,
and two women can wound,
pain is something we suffer alone.

So, I carve.
Once I tried to dance with gods,
straining to hold on to the promise offered.
Today I carve the space of empty hours,
doubting that what I make can ever be seen
as the smallest spark of light
in the radiance of the world's
love and beauty.

‘IF . . .’

If you can keep your feet when all around you
Are losing theirs and blaming it on you,
If you can push yourself when all men pace you
And make allowance for their racing too.
If you can force your heart and nerve and sinew
To serve your turn long after they have gone,
And so hold on when there is nothing in you
Except the will which says to them ‘Hold on!’

If you can race in crowds with strength renewed
Or run with Thames – nor lose the common touch,
If neither foes nor running friends can spike you,
If all men count with you, but none too much.
If you can fill the unforgiving minute
With sixty seconds’ worth of distance run,
You’ll win the race, beat everyone that’s in it
And – which is more – you’ll be a man, my son.

With apologies to Rudyard Kipling
My Captain’s speech at Thames Hare and
Hounds dinner for Oxford and Cambridge
cross-country teams

IN PRAISE OF RUMPLED BEDS

Here we are
like a Czar
- like a bar
(Whoops, gone too far)
I've been rumbled
you've been tumbled
bumble fumble
scrumble mumble
what a tangle
hard to handle
nerves a jangle
like a bangle
worlds collide
oceans wide
flooding tide
together
endeavour
never sever
passions fed
tousled head
rumpled bed
nuff said . . .

. . . peace

July 2019

THE WORDS I NEVER HEARD

A blackbird sings from the rooftop
and hears his call returned by another
across distance and time.
Even the silent sand murmurs
a quiet sigh as it is enfolded
by a wavelet.

But if a man
should shout into a void
and hear no faint echo
of his own calling,
the silence stabs his ears
and he is no more
than a pebble
among many others on the beach.

Could you have trusted me
without the words I spoke
of what you meant to me
when we lay close, touching?
For now, like the pebble,
I am deafened
by the words
I never heard.

October 2002

THE ROAD TO NOWHERE

This week we walked along
the Road to Nowhere.
Its tired tarmac top
pushed through
lonely, unkempt scrubland,
but each bramble-bordered curve
opened new possibilities.

Frosted crystals,
shattered shards of bottle-glass
caught by the autumn sun,
pretended to be diamonds
on the road's green mossy cushion.
And we walked together,
the past, the present
and the future.

The Road to Nowhere,
like a magic carpet,
started somewhere
and will carry us
over unknown lands,
towards our destination
– not Nowhere
but Everywhere.

After a walk with Anna Tamsin and her boys,
November 2012

HEAVEN'S LIGHT

Our lives are formed
by love of family, of friends,
by music and by art;
golden gifts of grace
revealed by God
to show men greatness.

Such gifts do not come cheap.
The shadows of those
who dare stand tall
fall long and contrast darkly
where light strikes gilt.

We have the love I need
before I leave
when I must dance
with gods;
that swirling dervish dance
across a fearsome void.

Hold on, hold on to love
or spin apart
to insignificance, insanity,
the nothingness
that frames creation.

(Cont.)

Or does heaven's light
truly lie behind
that pin-pricked shroud
and the grinding stones
of time?

Love then
thy neighbour as thyself,
and love with music, love with art,
but love with me as I love you.
Love life!
And we shall know ourselves
as truly human
– and divine.

For Victoria, January 2018

CHAPMANS' POOL

Together we pass
along the golden water's edge
as soft-spoken wavelets
advance to greet us.

Undecided, they retreat
and come again,
refreshing a palette
of love-lit stones
while the sun warmly approves.

Across the heaving upland
scented with springy turf,
we walk with minds entwined;
and teeter above the ancient chasm
and mystery of Chapmans' Pool.

We talk of families and friends,
of times that made us what we are.
And the listening gull
soars below us,
in this topsy-turvy world.

With the stones
we are washed
and lit anew.
For we, and the world, are richer,
when love takes its cue.

LIFE IS A PAPER BOAT

Life is a paper boat
set free on an immeasurable ocean;
buoyant and soaring
with the heaving peaks,
when a splashing crest
only refreshes and excites.

Through joyful sun and gloomy rain,
a paper boat travelling on and on
to deeper, deeper terra incognita.
Until, waterlogged by storms and
life's expectations, a splash is enough
to pause progress.

Slowly moving again,
labouring under the passing clouds,
striving onward until one day
a capsize,
and destiny is reached,
not destination.

But those who made it
and those who have seen it
know it has not sunk
in a Sargasso Sea
of indifference.
Its memory remains.

OUR TIME

The pendulum moves back and forth
to mark the path of Time.
But Time marches only in one direction,
he plays no games and never waits,
he dictates.

Time will destroy worlds – and viruses
in an endless moving flow.
We do not forget past Times and I cherish
the memories created in my Time with you,
and look forward to those in Times to come.

Time is so precious some do not wish to share it,
but it is ours to share.
Remember, there is Time for everything,
but we will not know it
until there is no more Time for anything.

2019

PARROT DROPPINGS – OLD CORN

I'm not averse
to writing in verse
cos words simply come to my mind.
The rub is that
(keep it under your hat)
the meaning's much harder to find.

The gleanings of meanings
from creative dreamings
are the fuel that powers my soul,
but what good is that
if it just comes out pat
when the goal is to keep off the dole?

Shape and form are the norm
when you work at your art,
but I need a gnat
if ideas are to begat
and I'm not to be just an old fart.

A gnat that can bite
and let in the light
that illumines the depths of my being;
to make sense of this vat
that stews under my hat
because I am looking – not seeing.

. . . *about carving and sculpture*

POEM WITHOUT WORDS

What will you do
when I have no fresh words
to speak of what
you mean to me?
Will you think
that all is done
and past,
that words repeated
lose the spicy warmth
that love revealed?
Shall we no longer
sing our lives
in harmony and laughter
but follow sad and solo lines?

Then, my muse,
my hands must warm
your heart,
my lips caress
your soul
and, as past and future
meet in our present,
we shall lie
close together,
two souls entwined
for all eternity.

SHARE WITH ME . . .

Share with me the sunset
and the sunrise.
Share with me a hillside
and the teardrop in your eye.

Sing with me a duet,
a sonnet never heard.
Sing with me a love song
and not in broken thirds.

Walk with me together,
hand-in-hand through sun and rain.
Walk and talk together,
never causing pain.

Lie with me and share with me,
close, so close, together.
Lie with me and love with me
together now
forever.

A CHRISTENING MESSAGE FOR NATHANIEL

A tiny, vital spark of life,
fanned with warmth
and love
by family and friends,
has grown to be
a steady burning flame
that will be called
Nathaniel.

No darkness
can extinguish
even the smallest spark
of your light,
for the light is love
and love is eternal,
transcending time
and place.

As you walk through life
Nathaniel,
shine out that love and light
so that the spirit
of those you meet
will come alight
and the world will be
a warmer, brighter place.

With great love, April 2010

THE SCULPTOR

As a blind man taps his line,
the carver's mallet taps through rings of time.
Through seven years,
through seven times seven,
and seven centuries more;
paring the tree of knowledge
to find the fruit
we should not eat.

In the silence of the night
feelings show themselves,
and dreams are spun
when the cold, dead moon
reels mocking around infinity.
The swinging mind cries out
that beauty conquers all,
but Nemesis then flirts her fan
and Darkness falls and hides
his tortured angel - man.

For we are wrapped in fantasy,
struggling for our grasped-at dreams
with slippery intuition,
haunted by failure to achieve our task.
By day our shavings fall,
staccato witness to a curling stream of consciousness.
And as I mould this wood
I know that it is shaping me.

(Cont.)

We make – not clever hopes
for cheap and superficial thrills,
we strive to give part of our soul
to the beseeching spirit
locked inside these grainy hills.
Through dreams transfigured by our hand,
we make not for ourselves alone,
but those like you who grasp
the handholds of the mind
that we have set across our time.
So that, together made immortal,
we declare that we were here
to those who come behind.

. . . Musing about carving, June 2009

A GUIDE TO CARVING SHAPES IN WOOD

Shapes
come in all sizes.
They may say nothing
or everything.
Sharp shapes, harsh, unforgiving,
or soft, flowing, loving.

Circling, spinning, twisting,
laying bare the complexity
of our fragile minds;
or tinted with space and light,
subtle, soft, ethereal,
seeking a path
beyond our knowing.

Wings, sails and swaying leaves
reveal the presence
of the wind
that sighs alone
across the hills.
The pattern of constant waves
reflects eternity.

A staccato lightning flash
contrasts the threat
of massive, looming
nimbus clouds.
A soaring skylark shows joy
and patience is revealed by a silent saint.

(Cont.)

In our world, mystic pyramids
and melting watches
form shapes that we can reveal
for others to share.

For I.J., a very talented carver, June 2013

SO CLOSE WE LIE

So close we lie
that my soul flies high
above dark clouds,
filled with the joy
of you.

In the wilderness
of my mind
you are a rose
fragrant as a summer eve;
soft petals – so easy to bruise –
red as the blood
that throbs through my heart.

Your silken body
whispers to mine;
your half-closed eyes
reveal your heart,
a glimpse of a soul
divine.

Tomorrow, you fly,
think of me
from time to time,
and us.
As I shall think of thee
with love and trust.

THE ASH TREE'S LEAF

Autumn waits for winter,
chill air dense and blue.
The ash tree's leaf
that in Spring burst into being
now trembles
like an old man's hands.
Rich in colour and desiccated,
cells past their sell-by date.

Once strong and
vibrant with promise,
knowing and growing
into maturity,
this ash leaf will become
just ash,
but its memory will sing and dance
in harmony
with those that come after.

IN THE LONG RUN . . .

Steel-slashed rain
and weeks of grey flannel clouds
give way to hard, dense air
washed pure and blue.
Today white rime sanctifies the land.
The life of trees falls still
and every moisture trace
glints diamond hard,
the tread of footfall treacherous.

Around the ancient hill fort's sheep-cropped rim
my feet mark my passing through this world
and through this time.
Along these springy, upland hills
I run with the buzzard
mewing his message of death in life.
My spirit flies higher still above this mortal day,
reaching to eternity with longing.

Running for home
the lengthening shadows
chart the fate of falling time,
and sun-struck jewels
flicker still in sombre hazel hedge.
My footsteps rhyme the cadence
of my breath and then, it seems,
they match the rhythm
of the universe.

(Cont.)

There is no time but this time,
no past and no future, for all is one and now.
Even the teeth of this east wind
cannot bite through time, it too will die.
Today I touched the mystery of this Gaia world,
Given through grace a princely glimpse of my soul
enfolded in eternity.
I knew understanding and saw peace.
Creation magnified my soul.

For the late John Bryant, fellow Thames Hare and Hounds member, my mentor, an associate and very good friend, who would understand. July 2020

THE THORN TREE

With bowed and sturdy limbs
twisted by its dance
with the elements and time,
and in silent accord with all
that shapes its world,
a tree can live a wisdom we sense,
but strive to find.

This thorn tree
has shared in confidence
your aches, your pain and the quiet, still,
most deep moments of your soul.
And as you rested upon it
you have become the slowly unfolding leaves
it offers to the world,
its gifts of love and beauty.

Together you sway,
strong, but still yielding,
sharp yet supple
as the satin-soft leaves of spring.
Together you pray,
reaching ever outward,
joined souls rising.
Together you sing the harmony of life.

(Cont.)

And I am but the wind
that drifts alone across the hills,
through the grasses
and over the shadows,
drawn to the gently beckoning leaves
of this thorn tree.
With leaves that clothe
its limbs with love.

In the soft silence of the evening,
we know the presence of each other.
Winter and summer, sun, sleet and rain,
we enfold, caress, forever,
no more weeping, no more pain,
the tree and thee
and life again.

THE BEE AND ME

Passing over the bonfire of my life
and the dark ashes
that lay on my soul,
I am drawn to the quiet buzz
of soft honeybees that,
indifferent to my presence,
work steadily
amid the dancing weeds.
Their working life redeems my soul,
while leaves and fruit from
the tall, dark tree fall quietly.
And together, the bees and me
share life,
again.

2016

A VALENTINE

My love,
no honeyed words
banal in red and gold:
no paeans of praise
for some anonymous amourette
will pad these lines
with sticky residue.

For I would speak of your charms,
of your grace and being,
of my wish to share with you,
to dance with you,
to sing with you,
to play with you
– to stay with you.

I cannot write of these
though I would whisper them
as incoherent words into your ear
as we lie close against each other,
giving and taking sacred pleasure
in who we are
and what we are together.

(Cont.)

We are bound, you and I,
by our tangled skeins
and by convention's chains.
Through good and ill they bind us still,
but we can tease and weave a love
into a strong, united bond,
my precious Valentine?

For Christine 2014

MY JITTERY VALENTINE

Here I sit
in Café Nero,
a white sheet of paper
staring at me
and my thoughts
drifting above like clouds
on a warm summer's day.

Winter could not be harsh,
because spring came early
with hints of warmth,
when I first met you
that November
my Jittery Valentine.

First attracted,
together we have grown
united and entwined,
a glorious tangle
of emotions and bodies,
of hopes and dreams,
to fill and be fulfilled.

Soon it will be summer
and we will walk
hand in hand
across the hills
with climbing skylarks,
drawn to the knowing warmth
of our own sun.

(Cont.)

For it is you that has made my days golden
and my nights red and purple.
The palette of my experiences
is enriched and more colourful
for knowing you.
Shall we see
what works we might create
if you will always be my Valentine?

For Jitterybug, 2015

ANOTHER VALENTINE

My lovely Valentine
Where will this special love
be led this special year?
We cannot know
but no longer will we look
through windows
at the lives of others.
For now we love again,
travelling together
among earth's treasures
in golden sun
and silver rain.

Through good and ill
we will share this world
as it turns and journeys
through the endless, cold universe.
And our love
will bring warmth and light
to our lives
and to the lives of others,
until fate plays its hand
and lays the final card.

For Christine Russell, 2017 (Printed in the programme for our Marriage Service the same year. And later read at Chris's funeral.)

A SMALL SAILING BOAT

This card will seem
a strange Valentine,
but not to me.
I was that small sailing boat you see
travelling across a grey, indifferent sea,
overshadowed by hills
and heading I knew not where.

And now climbing high
in a clear, empty sky is a
soaring vision of light and warmth,
inspiring my world
and banishing dark thoughts,
warming the shoots of love.

Now we have shared
so many sunrises and sunsets
that we know nights will pass
and we remain warm and safe
in the strength of our love,
until the day we share
our last sunset together.

Chris's Sailing Boat Valentine card, 2018

JUST MUSING . . .

In the late evening of my life
while I still see the sun and the light,
I know that my shadow is flowing
ever further
towards eternal darkness.

Written after Chris left.

WHEN YOU WALK UP TO ME

When you walk up to me,
when you look into my eyes,
when you talk to me,
when you touch me,
when you wake with me,
I know we have a shared love.

And now, if you will be my rainbow,
I will be your sun,
and my spirit
will soar across the heavens
from dawn to dusk.

My rays will light
the colours of your bow
and together we shall show
light and warmth
to this weary world
for ever.

Death shall not concern us
because as long as we exist
Death is not ours
and when he comes,
we no longer exist.

2017

TAKE ME WITH YOU

Go with my prayers
as your wings lift you
to trace the arc of the sky
towards the setting sun
and what will be.

Go with my thoughts
which lie side-by-side with you
under the wheeling stars,
and know how brief is our time
among these indifferent aeons.

Go with my arm around you
to share, to comfort, to caress,
to hold you through the night
until the soft new dawn
and promise of the day.

Go now with my love
and you do not travel alone.
Others may have loved you
but I am with you
and you are in my heart and soul.
Take me with you.

After Chris left, September 2021

Milton Keynes UK
Ingram Content Group UK Ltd.
UKHW040855181023
430815UK00002B/4